My Life Science Library

Animal Needs

Lisa J. Amstutz

Rourke Educational Media

A Division of Carson Dellosa Education

rourkeeducationalmedia.com

BEFORE AND DURING READING ACTIVITIES

Before Reading: *Building Background Knowledge and Vocabulary*

Building background knowledge can help children process new information and build upon what they already know. Before reading a book, it is important to tap into what children already know about the topic. This will help them develop their vocabulary and increase their reading comprehension.

Questions and Activities to Build Background Knowledge:

1. Look at the front cover of the book and read the title. What do you think this book will be about?
2. What do you already know about this topic?
3. Take a book walk and skim the pages. Look at the table of contents, photographs, captions, and bold words. Did these text features give you any information or predictions about what you will read in this book?

Vocabulary: *Vocabulary Is Key to Reading Comprehension*

Use the following directions to prompt a conversation about each word.
- Read the vocabulary words.
- What comes to mind when you see each word?
- What do you think each word means?

Vocabulary Words:
- *gills*
- *habitat*
- *predators*
- *shelter*

During Reading: *Reading for Meaning and Understanding*

To achieve deep comprehension of a book, children are encouraged to use close reading strategies. During reading, it is important to have children stop and make connections. These connections result in deeper analysis and understanding of a book.

Close Reading a Text

During reading, have children stop and talk about the following:
- Any confusing parts
- Any unknown words
- Text to text, text to self, text to world connections
- The main idea in each chapter or heading

Encourage children to use context clues to determine the meaning of any unknown words. These strategies will help children learn to analyze the text more thoroughly as they read.

When you are finished reading this book, turn to the last page for an **After Reading Activity**.

Table of Contents

Staying Alive

What does an animal need?

What helps it live and grow?

5

Basic Needs

Munch! All animals need food to eat.

Some eat plants. Others eat meat.

Do you get thirsty? Animals do too.

They need fresh water to drink.

Animals need clean air to breathe.

Some animals breathe with lungs. Others use **gills**.

gills

Animals must stay warm. But not too warm!

Some animals soak up the sun.
Others stay in the shade.

A Place to Live

Every animal needs a place to live.

An animal's home is called a **habitat**.

Animals need space to move and search for food.

Pounce!

Animals need **shelter** from the sun and storms.

They need a safe place to sleep.
Shh!

Prey animals must hide from **predators**. A bush or a hole can be a hiding spot.

Some predators hide to sneak up on prey!

Photo Glossary

gills (gilz): Organs near a fish's mouth that let it breathe by taking oxygen from water.

habitat (HAB-i-tat): The place where an animal or a plant is usually found.

predators (PRED-uh-turz): Animals that live by hunting and eating other animals.

shelter (SHEL-tur): A place that gives protection from bad weather or danger.

Make a Toad Home

Make a cozy toad home from an old flowerpot. Put it in a shady spot near your home or garden.

Supplies

clay flowerpot

paint or markers

trowel

shallow saucer

Directions

1. Decorate your pot with paint or markers.
2. Dig a hole in a damp, shady area with the trowel.
3. Lay the flowerpot on its side in the hole. Half of it should be underground.
4. Fill the bottom half of the pot with dirt. Pat it firmly.
5. Place the saucer nearby. Fill it with water. Wait for a toad to move in!

Index

About the Author

Lisa J. Amstutz is the author of more than 100 children's books. She loves learning about science and sharing fun facts with kids. Lisa lives on a small farm with her family, two goats, a flock of chickens, and a dog named Daisy.

After Reading Activity

Write a list of everything a person or an animal needs to survive. Then make up a song about the items on your list! Sing it to the tune of your favorite song.

Library of Congress PCN Data

Animal Needs / Lisa J. Amstutz
(My Life Science Library)
ISBN 978-1-73161-507-7 (hard cover)(alk. paper)
ISBN 978-1-73161-314-1 (soft cover)
ISBN 978-1-73161-612-8 (e-Book)
ISBN 978-1-73161-717-0 (e-Pub)
Library of Congress Control Number: 2019932050

Rourke Educational Media
Printed in the United States of America,
North Mankato, Minnesota

Edited by: Kim Thompson
Produced by Blue Door Education for Rourke Educational Media.
Cover and interior design by: Nicola Stratford

Photo Credits: Cover logo: frog © Eric Phol, test tube © Sergey Lazarev, cover tab art © siridhata, cover photo © Nick Biemans, cover title art © Vitaliy belozerov, page background art © Zaie; page 4-5 © clickit; page 6 © LouieLea, page 7 © Wild At Art; page 9 © symbiot; page 10 © Shevs, page 11 © Greg Amptman; page 12 © Jim Cumming, page 13 © samray; page 15 © Sergey Uryadnikov; page 17 © Kelp Grizzly Photography; page 18 © Kelp Grizzly Photography, page 19 © Coatesy; page 20 © Paul Reeves Photography, page 21 © Ethan Daniels   All images from Shutterstock.com